IELTS® Pathway to Success

A Strategic Exam Approach

Keith Kennedy

First published 2010

© Keith Kennedy 2014

Printed in the United States of America

The author and publisher of this book have made efforts to ensure its accuracy and make no representation to its completeness. The author and publisher shall in no event be held liable for any loss, damage or disruption caused by any errors or omissions.

All rights reserved. No part of this publication may be reproduced, stored in a retrieval system, or transmitted in any form or by any means without the prior written permission of the publishers or authors. Enquiries concerning reproduction outside those terms should be sent to the publishers.

Trademark Notice: Product or corporate names may be trademarks or registered trademarks, and are used only for identification and explanation without intent to infringe. IELTS is jointly owned by British Council, IDP: IELTS Australia and Cambridge English Language Assessment. Credits and acknowledgement of sources appear in the appropriate bibliographic pages at the end of this book.

Neutrino Publishing

neutrinopub@aol.com

ISBN 978-0-9938035-1-2

Contents

	Preface	Vii
1	**Introduction**	**9**

    To the Candidate
    Planning and Tips
    Keyword Strategies
    Listening Tip Strategies
    Reading Tip Strategies
    Personal Contract
    Essay Writing Tips and Strategies

2	**Vocabulary**	**17**

    Active and Receptive Divisions
    Vocabulary Practice

3	**Listening**	**27**

    Listening Skills Practice
    Introduction to IELTS Listening
    The Questions
    The Test
    Tips and Strategies for Listening
    Listening Summary Gap-Fill
    Shopping in Morocco and the US
    Different Ways to Express Numbers

4 Reading   37

Reading Skills Practice
Introduction to IELTS Reading
Academic Reading Module
General Training Module
Tips and Strategies for Reading
Skim Reading

5 Writing   49

Writing Skills Practice
Academic Writing Module
General Training Module
Academic Writing and General Module Task 2
Tips and Strategies for Writing
The Importance of Common Words used

6 Speaking   71

Speaking Skills Practice
Introduction to IELTS Speaking
Tips and Strategies for Speaking
IELTS Speaking Test Part 1
About Yourself
IELTS Speaking Test Part 2
IELTS Speaking Test Part 3

| 7 | Review & Memorising | 87 |

    Review to Strengthen Weaknesses
    Multisensory Review
    Sharpen Your Vocabulary Memory
    Enhance Grammar Understanding
    Past Paper Resources
    Teacher and Friend Resources

| 8 | Study Tips | 91 |

    Ten Days to Go
    Examination Day
    When Taking the Exam

| 9 | General Information | 95 |

    IELTS Preparation - Speaking Test
    Strategies for Speaking

| 10 | Speaking Exercises | 101 |

    IELTS Preparation Speaking Practice
    Paraphrasing Sentences
    Speaking Tasks
    Final Strategies

| 11 | Appendix 1 Answer Keys | 115 |

| 12 | Appendix 2 Resources | 123 |

    Bibliography   127

Preface

New to this Second Edition

The International English Language Testing System (IELTS) is part of a world-wide proficiency test for both education and immigration into English speaking countries.

Since the beginning of 2009 when I wrote the first edition of IELTS Pathway to Success, ideas for planning an approach when taking standardized tests came about. In this second edition, I have expanded upon the strategies and tips to help you study more efficiently. Minor changes have been made throughout the book to support current trends and ideas, that are both useful for the general and academic paths on the IELTS exam. I also reorganized the design and layout, and added an introduction section. Many sections remain unchanged because in the twenty-five year history of IELTS, the strategies, tips, and testing approach have proven to be successful in helping candidates move beyond their expectations.

The book is helpful for you as a candidate to understand the IELTS test procedure and how to avoid potential issues. When you know what to expect during the test, the process is less stressful and easier. The strategies and tips in this book will help guide your approach when responding to the four parts of the IELTS test questions.

Think of strategies and tips as part of your toolkit to help you maneuver through the IELTS exam. Learning how to use the tools described throughout this book efficiently can facilitate success and improve your band score. Thus, the central concept behind this book is its techniques to help YOU succeed. Good luck!

1
Introduction

Introduction

To the Candidate

Candidates use this book for academic, employment, and immigration tests into English speaking countries. The strategies utilized throughout the book have been designed to help improve your level of comprehension and skills. A strong cognitive commitment is essential in achieving success on the test. So making a personal study contract is your first priority to help manage your time on the examination. There is an example contract at the end of this introduction section. As you progress through the strategies, tips, and practice exercises included, you will have ample opportunities to make use of the skills gained.

Planning and Tips

The IELTS exam runs for two hours and consists of four parts: listening, reading, writing, and speaking, which have a number of different questions in each part.

Planning becomes essential for learning and memorising all the new vocabulary, grammar, structures, idioms, and skills being taught. A good **plan** requires a strategy to help you through the examination. This includes **tips** that will help you choose responses quickly. Whilst there are numerous methods to answer questions, you must find the method that is best for you. Strategies and tips help you make better decisions on the test. Remember to think cognitively, plan your steps, and have a strategy. A combination of these approaches will improve your time management on the test and increase exam results.

Plan
- what you need to do.
- your study time.
- your resources (Internet, dictionary, grammar book, CDs, and DVDs).
- your vocabulary, grammar, comprehension or production strategy.
- your review time.

Do
- your plan.
- your language learning or practice activities.

Review
- your work.
- why you did it.
- how well you did it.
- what you need to do next.

For key learning areas such as grammar, vocabulary, and communications skills, you should review what you have learnt on a regular basis. Remember: Plan, do, review, then plan, do, and review again.

Keyword Strategies

Strategies for identifying keywords on IELTS include searching for those words in the questions and answers followed by reading the passage. These keywords will provide you with a focus for reading and listening. When you identify keywords, you can respond to questions quickly and efficiently. Keywords can be compound nouns, nouns, verbs, and modifiers such as adjectives, or other words that change the meaning of a sentence. Keywords help to answer the who, what, where, why, and how questions. A good tip is to scan for many words simultaneously. What are keywords? What do you look for?

Keyword Identification
- multiculturalism is *not* a new idea.
- the IELTS test has *two* pathways.
- *all* humans desire companionship.
- new technology has *already* enhanced people's lives.

In the above short statements, the bold italic keywords reveal important information about their contextual meaning. The first example, '**not**' indicates a negative and shows that multiculturalism is an old idea. The second, '**two**' is a specific number that offers options for the IELTS test. The third, '**all**' determines that every human being desires relationships, and not just a few. Finally, '**already**' points to the existence of technology in people's lives, illustrating the past. Remember, always read the questions before proceeding with the reading or listening tasks. With the listening tasks, focus on the words before after the key words that add meaning to sentences.

Listening Tips and Strategies

Write no more than three words or a number
Before you listen to an audio on the test, read the incomplete sentences first. (The text is **not** provided during the test. The example below is for strategic purposes only) Pay attention to the underlined words that precede or follow the keywords in bold. **Tip**, keywords are often stressed. Remember, on the test you may be asked to write a limited number of words for each answer.

Questions
1: Plans are more than *strategies* for helping students
    A   they are road maps for 1 _____
    B   that 2 _____ one's position when teaching
    C   the position 3 _____ to learners' achievements

2: The essential constituents are
    A   a 1 _____ approach
    B   by 2 _____ objectives, the syllabus and core curriculum
    C   including the foundational 3 _____ of the learner

Planning and Evaluation
Plans are more than *strategies* for helping students, they are road maps for **direction** that **dictate** one's position when teaching, similar to Global Positioning Systems (GPS) that guide drivers. In classrooms, the 'position' **translates** to learners' achievements through **guided direction** of teachers. The essential constituents are a **focused approach** by **merging** objectives, the syllabus and core curriculum, including the foundational **needs** of learners.

Reading Tips and Strategies

Choose the correct answers
Read the questions first. Pay attention to the keywords that are bold. Now scan the article, identify the words and answer the questions.

Questions
1: The UK Government **enacted** significant **changes**
    A   around **September** 2007.
    B   before the **development and definitions** of teachers.
    C   after the LLUK **set out to raise** standards.

2: The LLUK **set out to raise** standards by
   A   **reforming** FE colleges.
   B   reducing **statutory** requirements
   C   asking teachers to **comply**.

Lifelong Learning UK

Around **September** 2007, the UK Government **enacted** significant **changes** to the education sector. These included **development and definitions** of a 'full teacher' and an 'associate teacher', as outlined by Lifelong Learning UK (LLUK). The LLUK **set out to raise** standards across the board by **reforming** Further Education (FE) colleges, making it a **statutory** requirement that all teachers are required to are obliged to **comply** with the new reforms.

Essay Writing Tips and Strategies

Planning Approach and Ideas

Planning your writing approach is essential for success on the IELTS test. Both the academic and general writing tasks have a minimum of 150, and 250 words respectively. The more you plan, the better and faster you can write. Set aside at least 5 minutes planning time for task 1 and 10 minutes for task 2, that still leaves you with plenty of time to write your essays.

Writing your thoughts and ideas on paper requires a cognitive process, whereby you analyse data and present your findings or arguments. But what to plan? Ideas, reasons and examples. Although vocabulary is not tested directly, planning your vocabulary enhances writing and expedites the process more efficiently. Ideas seem to flow readily when the words are in your head. Better vocabulary improves your overall score, for this reason vocabulary is included in this text.

Personal Study Contract

I .... will commit to studying for the IELTS exam as often as possible by using all resources available to me.

I am aware that improvement in my English ability is contingent upon frequent practice and diligent study.

I will commit to studying English .... hours each day.

I will listen to English at least .... hours each week.

I will read English at least .... hours per week.

I will write English at least .... hours per week.

I will speak English at least .... hours per week.

This contract constitutes a commitment with myself as I strive to reach an amazing IELTS Band score. I will adhere to the terms that I have set for myself.

Name ....

Date ....

1
Vocabulary

Vocabulary

Active and Receptive Vocabulary Divisions

The human brain has two divisions for vocabulary. There is a fairly small active vocabulary base for everyday speaking and writing, and a larger receptive vocabulary base used to understand listening and reading. However, the receptive vocabulary is not used productively.

This is also the case with your mother language and in English. In preparation for this part of the exam try to increase your active and receptive vocabulary levels. To increase your receptive vocabulary levels read and listen to English as often as possible. Begin with familiar topics and then move on to less familiar ones. In a similar way, you can increase your active vocabulary level simply by writing all the new words down that you come across during lessons and homework assignments. Try organising new vocabulary into specific groups such as subject or grammatical form. In addition, use new vocabulary as soon as possible when speaking or writing. An important point to remember is not to worry about any mistakes. Your language skills can only improve if you try your best.

    A good **strategy** for increasing vocabulary levels is to transform words. For example: from the noun '**force**' you can learn the word '**workforce**', '**counterforce**', '**enforcement**', '**forceps**'.

    The Longman Essential Activator categorizes words by their specific meaning, so from an easy word like '**walk**' you can learn '**stroll**', '**stride**', '**step**', '**tiptoe**', or '**wander**'. Remember that English utilizes a variety of fixed expressions, so try to expand your work by avoiding single words. The Longman and Cambridge dictionaries provide good examples of words used in expressions. Review the entry for 'press'. How many examples are there?

Vocabulary Practice

Describing & Analysing Tables or Graphs

Match the words from column 1 with the word or phrases from column 2 that mean closely the same thing. Write the corresponding letter (A to J) in the box provided on the left.

Column 1				Column 2

	Column 1	Column 2
	1. plunge	A. theatrical
	2. discrepancy	B. equable
	3. considerable	C. slump
	4. slightly	D. a steep and rapid fall
	5. dramatic	E. precipitously
	6. increase	F. abatement
	7. constant	G. marginally
	8. sharply	H. momentous
	9. decline	I. aggrandize
	10. reduction	J. variance

Words Related to Media

Match the words from column 1 with the words or phrases from column 2 that mean closely the same thing. Write the corresponding letter (A to J) in the box provided on the left.

Column 1   Column 2

Column 1	Column 2
1. sitcom	**A.** small format newspapers
2. broadsheets	**B.** a printed statement about somebody that is not true; slander
3. soap opera	**C.** a regular programme on T.V. that shows the same characters in different amusing situations
4. tabloids	**D.** venal
5. libel	**E.** .newspapers that print a lot of shocking stories about people's private lives
6. paparazzi	**F.** a story about the lives and problems of a group of people, which is broadcast every day on television or radio
7. documentary	**G.** .large format newspapers
8. gutter press	**H.** photographers
9. photography	**I.** a film or television programme giving facts about something
10. unscrupulous	**J.** cheap and of poor quality

Words Related to Work or Employment

Match the words from column 1 with the words or phrases from column 2 that mean closely the same thing. Write the corresponding letter (A to J) in the box provided on the left.

Column 1   Column 2

	Column 1	Column 2
	1. downsize	A. coloured sticky paper used for notes that is easily removed
	2. post-it	B. self-employed
	3. chore	C. connected with people who do physical work in industry
	4. redundancy	D. a task that you do regularly
	5. free lance	E. a period of time when someone stops work to study or travel
	6. white-collar	F. an act of making people unemployed because there is no more work left
	7. blue-collar	G. connected with low-paid jobs done mainly by women, like offices jobs
	8. lay-off	H. when somebody has to leave their job because there is no work
	9. pink-collar	I. working in an office, rather than in a factory
	10. sabbatical	J. to reduce the number of people who work in a company, business, etc. in order to reduce costs

Words Related to Money & Finance

Match the words from column 1 with the words or phrases from column 2 that mean closely the same thing. Write the corresponding letter (A to J) in the box provided on the left.

Column 1   Column 2

	Column 1	Column 2
	1. extravagant	A. a printed record of money paid, received, etc
	2. mortgage	B. much too high
	3. bankrupt	C. money that you owe to a bank when you have spent more money than is in your bank account
	4. inflation	D. a special kind of loan used to buy a house over a period of time
	5. building society	E. somebody's house value that is less than the amount of money that is still owed to a bank
	6. overdraft	F. a bank instruction to allow money to be taken from your account on a particular date
	7. direct debit	G. spending a lot more than you can afford or than is necessary
	8. exorbitant	H. an organization that lends people money to buy a house
	9. negative equity	I. a state of economy where prices and wages increase
	10. statement	J. without enough money to pay what you owe

Words Related to Business & Finance

Match the words from column 1 with the words or phrases from column 2 that mean closely the same thing. Write the corresponding letter (A to J) in the box provided on the left.

Column 1　　　　　　　　　Column 2

	Column 1	Column 2
	1. net	A. a person who makes money by starting or running businesses
	2. state-owned	B. amount of money that remains when nothing more is to be taken
	3. VAT	C. a state of inactivity in business
	4. entrepreneur	D. a state of economy where prices and wages are rising to keep pace with each other
	5. stagnation	E. industry or a company under the control of the government
	6. GNP	F. a difficult time for a country when there is less trade activity, that results in unemployment
	7. GDP	G. the total amount of something before anything is taken away
	8. inflation	H. the value of goods and services produced by a country in one year
	9. gross	I. a tax that is added to the price of goods and services
	10. recession	J. the value of goods and services produced by a country in one year, including foreign income

Words Related to Geography

Match the words from column 1 with the words or phrases from column 2 that mean closely the same thing. Write the corresponding letter (A to J) in the box provided on the left.

	Column 1	Column 2
	1. summit	A. an area of land that is fairly flat and not very high above sea level
	2. plateau	B. a large area where towns have joined together, often around a city
	3. lowlands	C. land shaped like a triangle, where a river has split into several smaller rivers that enters the sea
	4. peninsula	D. a large mass of ice formed by snow, moving slowly on mountains
	5. conurbation	E. the condition of having reduced numbers of inhabitants or none
	6. depopulation	F. an area of low land between hills or mountains
	7. delta	G. an area of flat land that is higher than the land around it
	8. sprawl	H. the highest point of something, especially the top of a mountain
	9. glacier	I. land that is almost surrounded by water but is joined to a larger piece of land
	10. valley	J. an act of spreading to cover a large area in an untidy way

Words Related to Architecture and Housing

Match the words from column 1 with the words or phrases from column 2 that mean closely the same thing. Write the corresponding letter (A to J) in the box provided on the left.

Column 1   *Column 2*

	Column 1	Column 2
	1. porch	A. large country house surrounded by land that belongs to it
	2. maisonette	B. land or buildings not used or cared for and, in bad condition
	3. attic	C. a building made in sections that can be put together later
	4. facade	D. a house that is one of a row of houses that are joined together on each side
	5. prefabricated	E. a platform with an open front and a roof, built onto the side of a house on the ground floor
	6. eyesore	F. joined to another house by a wall on one side that is shared
	7. semi-detached house	G. a building, an object, etc. that is unpleasant to look at
	8. derelict	H. the front of a building
	9. terraced house	I. a flat with rooms on two floors of a building with separate entrances
	10. manor house	J. a room or space just below the roof of a house, often used for storing things

3
Listening

Listening

Listening Skills Practice

Predict
Try to understand as much about the topic before you listen. Ask yourself questions about the speakers and what they are likely to say. Prepare yourself for listening by having lots of questions and predictions in your mind. Be prepared to change those predictions as you listen.

Prepare
Read the questions before you listen and think about the sort of answers which might be possible.

As you listen
When you listen, you can make notes of any key words or information. If you can't write down names, write the initial letters. Read through your notes, and try to predict the words or names before you 'fill the gaps' on the answer sheet. **Tip**, key words are often stressed. Listen for increased intonation during the test.

Listen for clues
Listen, not only to the information but also to the voices. Are they angry or happy? Sincere or joking? Are they female or male speakers? Are they young or old?

Listen frequently

Listening is a skill which improves with a lot of practice.

Introduction to IELTS Listening

This is the first part of the IELTS exam. The test last 30 minutes and the format consists of 4 sections with a total of 40 questions, which are worth one mark each. At the start of the test you are given two papers - a question paper and an answer sheet. As you listen to the recording, you should write your answers in the spaces on the question sheet. The examiner will give you time later to transfer these to the answer sheet.

The Questions

In the listening section, you will have approximately 30 seconds to review the questions before the recording begins. (You need this time to understand what information to listen for.) The recording is played once only, so if you miss any information during this time you will not have another opportunity to hear it again. The accents and voices that you hear could be Australian, British, or Canadian, so remember there are numerous differences between them. (For example, an Estuary English accent from South East England sounds different from an East London accent.)

The recording always begins with an introduction that outlines the background information you are going to hear. Then you will hear the instructions and what you have to do with the information.

The question types might be any of the following listed below. Although the descriptions may appear slightly confusing initially, these become clearer once you have tried a few practice tests.

Classification
Occasionally you have:
- different types of lists to sort into specific groups of people.
- to identify information from two different lists, for example, names and addresses.

Completing notes or a diagram
Occasionally you have to:
- place words in different areas.
- select a word from a list.
- match different parts of lists such as names and addresses.
- label parts of a diagram or map.

Multiple choice
Occasionally you:
- might need to select one answer.
- need to select the correct picture or diagram.
- must select more than one answer to gain a mark.
- must select more than one answer and each answer is worth a mark.

Short answers
Usually these are one word or a number, but sometimes you need three words. Keep in mind that numbers count as words, so 24, or twenty-four is a single word.

Short answers might also be answers by themselves, or you might need to use an answer to complete a sentence.

The Test

The four parts of the test are divided into two conversations, and two monologues. They are also divided into social situations and training/educational situations. So you will get a social conversation and a social monologue, and a training/educational conversation and a training/educational monologue.

Part 1. This is a social conversation, usually dealing with a 'transaction'. This might include someone asking for information or buying something. You will need to listen for keywords or specific information like names or prices.

Part 2. This monologue is something you might come across in everyday situations, such as a public announcement, or someone giving instructions about how to do something, or describing a particular situation. Again you need to listen for factual details.

Part 3. This section is a conversation about education or training. For instance, you might hear a conversation between a teacher and student discussing exam results, or someone asking for a more detailed explanation. Parts 3 and 4 are often considered the most challenging by candidates because you not only have to listen for facts, but also peoples' opinions.

Part 4. This component is an academic monologue. The speaker will be presenting an argument or giving an explanation for something. (Note: an argument in an academic context is not a verbal fight, but the thoughts and ideas to help reach a conclusion.) Your task is to understand the argument, specific facts and ideas presented, and the conclusion revealed by the speaker.

Tips and Strategies for Listening

Listen to a lot of English on the radio. Also listen to music in which the words of the songs are clear. Songs are a good way of learning the rhythm of a language, as the timing of a song is often an exaggerated form of the timing of everyday speech.

Train yourself to listen for specific information during radio interviews. When watching films, try to predict what people might say in a certain situation. Listen for signs that information is about to be given (for example 'please remember that ...', 'I advised you not to ...). When questions are posed train yourself to understand immediately what response is expected, such as a place, time or number.

When you get the question paper read it carefully. Look for types of answers you might need. Look for keywords, and clues about what you can expect to hear.

Don't skip over the instructions. Check carefully that know what you are supposed to do with each question. Make sure you know what type of answer is required.

When you are listening, if you hear something useful, like a name being spelled, write it down at once, even if you can't immediately work out what you will do with the information.

Keep up with the recording. If you find that you are more than ten seconds behind, skip some answers instead of trying to rely on your memory. (The information usually comes in the same order as the questions.)

Listen for changes in decisions or corrections by people. Occasionally this means that you will have to revise your answer.

In addition, listen for synonyms (words with similar meaning) or speakers giving you answers in an unfamiliar way, such as when an answer on a multiple-choice section is 'twelve' the speaker on the recording might respond by saying 'a dozen'.

At the time you transfer your answers to the answer sheet, take a moment to check for inappropriate responses or errors. Nonetheless, if in doubt, go with your instinct and leave your original answer. Candidates that take the IELTS exam often change correct answers to incorrect ones. Try to answer all the questions and when you are not sure, use your instincts. An answer is better than no answer, because it might be correct.

Listening - Summary Gap-Fill

Often listening exercises involve listening to a short passage to complete a gap-fill exercise. Take a look at the following questions for the short passage comparing shopping in Morocco and the US.

Questions
1: How different is shopping for food in Morocco from the US?
    A   it is very different
    B   it is quite different
    C   it is slightly different

2: Where do people shop in Marrakech?
    A   in small local shops
    B   at a farm
    C   in an open-air market

3: In general, is food fresher in Marrakech or the US?
    A   food is fresher in Marrakech
    B   food is fresher in the US
    C   food is fresh in both countries

4: Which country is more expensive, Morocco or the US?
- **A** Morocco is cheaper
- **B** the US is more expensive
- **C** the prices are the same

5: What does it mean to bargain?
- **A** it means to negotiate the terms of a sale
- **B** it means to argue with the seller
- **C** it means to get something for free

6: When food prices are unchangeable, what does this mean?
- **A** they are flexible
- **B** they are the same
- **C** they are fixed

Now complete the summary gap-fill exercise below. Choose the correct letter, A, B, or C from above, locate the key word or words (more than one answer may be possible). Write no more than three words for each space in the text. **Tip**, connected words that make adjectives such as **blue-green** lake, count as one word. Remember, the word or words must make the sentence grammatically correct.

Shopping in Morocco and the US
In general, shopping for food in Morocco is 1 _____ from shopping in the United States (US). First of all, in Marrakech you buy most of the food in an 2 _____ whereas in the US it's bought in stores. Second, food is much 3 _____ and cheaper in Marrakech, but in the US it's not as fresh and 4 _____. In addition, in Marrakech you can 5 _____ the price of food, but in the US prices are nearly always 6 _____ .

Remember, as a **strategy**, identify keywords in the questions. **Tip**, these words in the listening exercise are often stressed.

Listening for numbers

Numbers form part of the IELTS listening test, which consists of telephone, addresses, dates, other kinds of numbers. Focusing on numbers carefully can help get you a higher band score.

Avoid the pitfalls

Frequently you will hear more than one number, but the first number may not be the one you need. In some cases, the speaker can provide information and then retract it or change it. **Tip**, write down numbers when you hear them. With longer numbers, listen carefully for a falling intonation which usually indicates the last number. The **strategy** here is to be familiar with the various ways to express numbers.

Different Ways to Express Numbers

International phone numbers: +44 20 8291 9274
Plus forty-four, twenty, eighty-two, ninety-one, ninety-two seventy-four.
Plus four four, two zero eight, two nine one, nine two seven, four.
Dates: July 12, 2014
July twelfth, two thousand and fourteen
July twelve, twenty fourteen
Prices: £ 15.60
Fifteen pound and sixty pence.
Fifteen sixty

Look in the appendix section for additional resources online.

4
Reading

Reading

Reading Skills Practice

Do not let difficult vocabulary slow down your reading. Just ignore the difficult vocabulary on your first reading and understand as much as you can.

Usually the first sentence in a paragraph provides you with a general idea about the paragraph theme. Therefore, it is important to carefully review the question words. Look at the following inquiry words and the kind of information you need to give for each one: **where** - needs a location, **how long** - needs a reference to time or distance, **why** - needs a rationale, **when** - needs a specific time, **who** - needs a person's name. Inspect the reading task carefully after your initial scanning. Carefully inspect the reading task after your initial reading. These tasks might require a general or comprehensive understanding, while other tasks may necessitate more specific information that you have to search for.

Learn to '**skim**' – that is to read through the whole text quickly to get a general idea of the meaning. Learn the skill of '**scanning**' the text looking for key words. Then read around the key word to find the answer. If the task requires detailed understanding, read the questions carefully and have a clear idea in your mind of what you are looking for before you read the text a second time.

Don't be afraid to read the text a third or fourth time to get the information and ideas you need. This is much better than 'inventing' your answers. **Remember** that fast, repeated reading is much more effective than slow, careful reading. When doing practice tests, keep track of your time and try to divide your time equally. In general the reading passages go from easy to difficult, so it's a good idea to spend less time on the first two and more on the last one.

Introduction to IELTS Reading

The reading part of the exam runs for one hour. There are 40 questions and three sections that you have to complete. For each correct answer you get one point. You must write your responses on the answer sheet only, which is separate from the passages and questions on the test paper. If you mistakenly write your responses on the question paper first, there will be insufficient time to transfer them over later. Also keep in mind that bad grammar and spelling will lose you points.

Unlike other language exams, the IELTS is more diverse with different categories of questions and reading tests that can change. The instructions form part of the test, so it is imperative to read them carefully. Even though you might have little time remaining.
do not attempt to answer the questions until you know what you need to do.

The questions may also consists of various types. For example, with multiple-choice questions you usually have four options to select from, or on the other hand you might be asked according to a statement presented whether the information is true, false, or not given. In addition, you might have to complete a gap-fill (write missing words in a sentence) or write short answers. Remember, check carefully for the maximum number of words that you can write, which includes conjunctions, prepositions and articles. You might also be asked to select titles for the different parts of the text, fill in a chart or a table, or locate answers in a paragraph. (Remember when looking for information the paragraphs might use synonyms or other words that are not used in the questions, but the paragraphs will be numbered.) Sometimes you need to name the paragraph when the writer provides an opinion on something. In this case and with searching for answers, there might be an option to select 'information not given' in the paragraphs.

In each of the paragraphs, the questions types might consist of one, two, three or four of the above. Invariably, there are at least two types.

Always review the questions before any reading exercise. Then when you recognise possible key information, you can go back to the paragraphs and begin answering the questions. Time management is always a problem for candidates in the IELTS reading so avoid dividing the time into three equal parts of 20 minutes, but instead allocate less time to the first section (16-18 minutes) and a little more to the last section (20-23 minutes).

The reading is either the Academic or the General Training module. You cannot mix up your modules and take (for instance) the General Training reading module and the Academic writing module. When you enroll to do the exam, you must say whether you are doing the General Training of the Academic version of the exam, and you will only do the reading from the version you have selected. Therefore you only need to read the information about both modules if you are not sure which version of the exam you want to do. Otherwise, you only need to look at the information about your version of the exam.

Academic Reading Module

There are three passages which together contain between 2,000 and 3,000 words, though the three passages will not all be the same length.

For example, there might be one passage that displays a diagram or a graph with very little text and you will need to answers questions that test your understanding of the information presented (you will be provided with an explanation for any technical or unusual words).

Another passage might contain information from a book or magazine. This is authentic material (real material that was published) and is usually chosen from topics that would interest university students, or is the kind of information that students must read as part of their curriculum.

One passage is invariably based on an argument. Remember, an 'argument' in an academic context means an opinion about something, and the writer is attempting to prove that the opinion is right. It is not important whether you agree or disagree with the writer's opinion, but the questions test your understanding of what the writer is attempting to say and how the opinion is proven.

With all the passages, you need to make sure that you understand what the text is about and how it is put together. (i.e. Whether it is a narrative, an argument, or presenting facts.)

General Training Reading Module

Whereas the three excerpts in the academic section might have two passages and a diagram or graph, in the General Training module each of the three sections might have various shorter texts.

In section 1 there are two or three texts. These texts generally relate to your understanding of the kind of information needed to live in an English-speaking country. For instance, you may get specific instructions that often appear on signs, in advertisements, or instruction manuals. There might also be passages from magazines or books. Before you can answer the questions you will need to understand phrases like idiomatic expressions and headline news articles in English, because you have to prove that you can locate important key pieces of information.

The second section is usually slightly harder, so you should allocate more time. Invariably you will have one or two texts, often these are from an instruction manual or a employee handbook for a company that might outline certain procedures.

In most cases section three is one text. Commonly, it is the kind of reading you might come across in a magazine. Usually this is a kind of narrative or a descriptive representation of something, although it can also be an interview. Remember that this section is quite often more difficult, so it is important to allow extra time to complete the task.

Tips and Strategies for Reading

The reading tips and strategies below help with your cognitive thinking process. This process is essential for effective training in IELTS reading. A good way to build reading skills is to focus on short articles in newspapers or magazines that interest you, these are excellent resources as they often reflect the topics in IELTS.

Try to read copious numbers of English articles before the exam, as this will give you confidence when faced with unfamiliar words.

Since IELTS reading texts vary in length there is little time to read carefully, so you must train yourself to read efficiently and quickly. The **strategy** here is to quickly for general meaning and scan for keywords, dates, or phrases. Read the sentences where the words or dates are found, and check for related words or paraphrasing before and after the information.

Tip, look for italic or capitalized words. Be aware that paraphrasing may have an identical meaning to the words in the text, so your understanding of the context is important.

Don't try to read the entire text in detail, only focus on the parts where the words or phrases in the questions are similar. Remember, this is why reading the questions first is important to gain insight into the context of the text.

Time management and a definitive strategy will help you complete the exam on time. As such, you will need a plan and a general idea what is best for you. Think about the following:

Think about
- the time spent on reading text.
- the amount of time for each question.
- how long to spend on each group of questions.
- the remaining time at the end to answer missed questions.

Remember that focusing on the questions before you answer is imperative, as words that may appear similar could in fact be quite different. For example, 'always' or 'often' are different degrees of frequency. Make sure you understand these differences and check the answers before you respond to them. Now try the following exercise.

Skim Reading

Questions - London Congestion Charge
Take a look at the following questions for the London Congestion Charge and try to get an idea of what answers you will need after reading.

1: This article tells you about a charge that has been around since:
- A   January 2003.
- B   February 2003.
- C   March 2003.
- D   April 2003.

2: This article doesn't give information about:
- A   people who are exempt from paying the charge.
- B   how London's residents were consulted about the charge.
- C   the roads that form the boundaries of the zone.
- D   the process to check whether drivers have paid the congestion charge.

3: Is there more than one way to pay the Congestion Charge?
- A   Yes.
- B   No - the method of payment depends on where you live.
- C   No - everyone has to pay online.
- D   Yes - but you cannot change you preferred method of payment once you have chosen.

4: Does the article inform the reader about why the charge was introduced?
- A   Yes.
- B   No.

5: This text is aimed at:
- A   businesses.
- B   students.
- C   London residents.
- D   everyone.

6: What type of text is this?
- A   Descriptive.
- B   Instructive.
- C   Informative.
- D   Persuasive.

7: How does the text suggest that you can find out more about the London Congestion Charge?
- A   Speak to your local MP.
- B   Write a letter to Transport for London.
- C   The text doesn't say.
- D   Call a telephone number or visit a website.

8: Can you find out about different methods that are being used to check whether drivers have paid the congestion charge?
- A   No.
- B   Yes.

9: Are maps of the congestion zone available to the public?
- A   Yes, and this text tells you where you can get them.
- B   Yes, but this text doesn't say where you can get them from.
- C   No, maps aren't available.
- D   The text doesn't say.

10: This text does give information about:
- A   the weather in London.
- B   the number of drivers who evade paying the charge each day.
- C   the days and times the Congestion Charge applies.
- D   the names of shops where you can get Congestion Charge maps.

London Congestion Charge

Ken Livingston, the mayor of London, introduced the Congestion Charge on Monday 17 February 2003 to convince people to use public transport rather than their cars because of the high pollution levels in Central London.

The congestion zone comprises of roads such as Pentoville Road, Great Eastern Street, Kennington Lane and Park Lane. These roads in the north, east, south and west respectively, make up the circular route around Central London. Maps for the congestion zone are available in the press, from selected outlets and online.

Drivers have to pay £11.50 each day they wish to travel through or within the charge zone between the hours of 07.00 and 18:00, Monday to Friday. Drivers have a choice about how they pay the £11.50. They can pay online, via the Internet, phoning, texting on their mobile phones and over the counter at petrol stations and convenience stores. Commuters also have a choice about how often they wish to pay. They can pay daily, weekly, monthly or annually.

Not everyone has to pay the £11.50. Those exempt include the emergency services, registered-disabled drivers, taxis and those using alternative energy vehicles. These people or organisations have to apply for exemption, which can be done online. Registered residents receive a 90% discount.

The circular zone is monitored by over 600 cameras, and across the whole network as cars enter or leave the Central London zones. The cameras check car number plates to verify whether owners have paid or whether they have exemptions. Except for those that are exempt, drivers have until 24:00 hours to settle the charges otherwise a penalty notice will be sent to the registered owner of the car. Owners that fail to pay charges will be levied additional penalties or have their vehicle removed.

For more information, call 0845 900 1234 or visit Transport for London's Congestion Charge website at http://tfl.gov.uk/modes/driving/congestion-charge.

5
Writing

Writing

Writing Skills Practice

Plan a strategy and learn the techniques of 'process writing'. Don't pick up your pen and then start to think what to write. Keep in mind that that task 1 requires a minimum of 150 words and at least 250 words for task 2. You will need to spend about 20 minutes on task 1 and 40 minutes on task 2.

Collect your ideas and make notes
Think about the reader. Ask yourself "What does the reader need to know?" "What does the reader know already?" Think about the 'communicative purpose' of what you are writing.

Organise your notes into a logical structure
Think about the language you will need, and try to avoid informal or colloquial language. As you organise your structure, recognise what 150 or 250 words looks like. Remember, these are the minimum word counts.

Write your first draft
Try leaving every other line blank so you can make corrections without having to rewrite the whole text. You will not have time during the test to rewrite. Spend some time reviewing and correcting your writing to ensure that it has a logical flow.

Imagine you are the reader
Check your draft contains all the information the reader needs and that it is clearly expressed. Also check for language mistakes and correct them. Use one idea for each paragraph you write and try not to repeat words, use synonyms.

Learn from the corrections your teacher gives you
Identify your bad habits and frequent mistakes. Watch out for spelling, grammar, and punctuation errors as you will lose marks for these. Concentrate on correcting your writing structures and grammatical errors to gain a higher score.

Learn how to check your own writing
Remember to look for a logical structure and development. Look for well-organised paragraphs. Look for details – spelling, punctuation, word order. Learn from your fellow students' mistakes. Your teacher can help you do this in class. **Avoid using ideas from the model answer, as this will result in an invalid test.**

Introduction to IELTS Writing

Both the IELTS writing tasks for the Academic and General Training modules run for one hour. The first task is comparatively shorter, and candidates must write at least 150 words. As the paper for this task carries a thirty-percent mark, you should limit your time to 20 minutes including preparation. For the second task you need to write a minimum of 250 words, and spend the last 40 minutes to complete it.

With both tasks, it is important to make sure that you understand what you have to do before you start writing. You can make notes on the question paper to help you to plan exactly what you are going to write on the answer sheets.

Remember your writing must represent a clear and coherent statement of what you want to express, examiners want to see a logical flow to your writing. Therefore, your response needs to address all the required points, going from one logical thought to another using numerous connecting words or phrases such as firstly, secondly, and, as well as, it follows that and so on.

Keep in mind that you will get more points for using an appropriate range of sentence structures and vocabulary, but not if you go to extremes and use too many language patterns in one paragraph.

Also, if your essays do not meet the minimum of 150 and 250 words, or are too long, you will lose points. In addition, when repeating information from the question, ensure that you paraphrase it. If you make a writing error, don't waste time trying to erase it, just draw a single line through the incorrect words then continue with the correction.

Academic Writing Module

Task 1

In this task you must write a succinct analysis of some graphical information into an essay format. This information is usually a chart, graph or a table. (Charts and graphs reflect trends or changes in different kinds of information. These data might also show various results for each situation and outcome.) The purpose for these visual representations is to test a candidate's ability to describe data using appropriate language that identifies the most important items. The examiners want to ascertain your understanding of the information given. Preferably, spend a little time ensuring that you interpret what the graphical information is showing, try not to be overly concerned with any technical words, but instead write a short statement of what you see. Generally, writing a description about the question in the first sentence is a good idea. (For instance, 'This information describes the number of people that buy lunch at a convenience store, what kind of food they buy, and how much they spend.' or 'This describes how to set up a new computer and connect the various pieces of hardware together.') The important point to remember is that you must present and summerise the information as opposed to giving an opinion.

General Training Module

Task 1
In most cases for task 1 you will write a letter about a particular situation and be instructed on what the situation is, such as asking someone to attend a meeting. You will have to provide information from three-summerised bullet points, so paraphrase your letter carefully. Pay attention to the question and the tense that you should use. For example, you would need a future tense for the above scenario, whereas in a situation such as thanking friends for a lovely party, would require a past tense. Remember, it is essential that you address all the bullet points, and structure your letter in a concise and logical manner.

Academic Writing and General Training

Task 2
This writing task is a discursive piece. This task requires a structured composition for both Academic and General Training modules where you must give a constructive analysis to support an opinion, or present your own point of view. For instance, you may have to discuss and present arguments for the following comment: 'These days people and society have too much wealth'. Whatever the topic argument, be ready to give your point of views and justify them, or even confront contrary

views. In addition, you may have to find the cause of a problem or suggest a solution. Remember the key question might also have a secondary sub-question, so in the scenario above you might have to discuss the issues of money and society.

The examiner gives points to candidates who concisely demonstrate their argument, not on the examiner's opinions. Assessment will be on a range of grammatical structures, vocabulary and ability to organise a case logically. In the General Training module, candidates can depict their views and opinions based on experiences and anecdotes.

In the first instance begin by summarising the argument. Next, briefly express your key points contrary to the opinion. Then prove these points are wrong, support your opinion with several sentences, and write a summary of the main issue and action to take. For instance, a discursive paper on 'Will future technology mean that one day people might use computers to prepare meals' may conclude with 'As a result, despite how good computers become, people will still want a fresh homemade meal'. Remember, this task is 20-minutes long.

Tips and Strategies for Writing

The writing tips and strategies below can help you think logically and cognitively. The first **tip** to keep in mind is time. Remember, task 1 has a twenty-minute limit so plan, write, and revise your response during this time. When thinking about your structural layout for task 1, try to allow about 4 minutes each for your statement and description, and 12 minutes for the trends and characteristics part. (This is your overview of the chart or graph.) As a quick **strategy**, you can paraphrase your initial statement from the task 1 instructions. This must contain the details and nature of the chart or graph. Remember, all of the following elements must be present: initial statement, analyses of data presented, and a word count of between 150-175. Too few, or too many words will lose you points!

For task 2 there is a forty-minute time frame in which you need to plan, write, and revise. In task 2 you will need an introduction, main body, and conclusion. Divide your time up into these approximate time frames: 8 minutes for the introduction, 20 minutes for the main body, 5 minutes for the conclusion, and 7 minutes reviewing and checking for grammatical errors.

Read task 2 instruction carefully, as you might be asked to compare, describe, or provide an opinion about something. **Tip** - planning is the key to writing. Do not pick up a pen and write. Cognitively think about the questions and information needed to complete the task. Ensure all elements are in place, 'introduction', 'main body', and 'conclusion'. Remember, as a **strategy** you can paraphrase task 2 instructions. (Paraphrase means to state the same idea in your own words. For example, 'In your opinion, should universities teach languages to students as part of their academic programmes?' Paraphrased as 'It is imperative for universities to instruct students in one or more languages, because of the need in the global economy'.) When paraphrasing, ensure you use synonyms, and keywords to restate the question. In the final sentence of your introduction, you will need a thesis statement. This statement reflects your ideas to support your arguments in the main body of your text.

Task 1

Take a look at the following academic model answer for the London Borough of Greenwich Budget. Pay attention to the keywords used and notice how all the main points have been covered.

Write a report describing the changes that took place. You must write at least 150 words in 20 minutes.

Model Answer London Borough of Greenwich Budget

The two charts compare the budget for the London Borough of Greenwich in both 1980 and 1990 and that the largest expenditure was on education. Roads, parks, and building facilities remained at much the same levels. On the other hand, there was a dramatic rise in government salaries which doubled it percentage over the ten-year period.

Education made up the largest percentage of the budget costs, although the percentage decreased slightly by 9% from 42% in 1980 to 33% in 1990. Park maintenance in 1990 was the second largest expenditure, increasing its proportion of the budget cost to 27% from 22% in the previous decade. Roads, the second largest expenditure in 1980 at 26%, decreased in costs slightly to 25% and provided a small saving ten years later. There was no change in the percentage of building facilities, which remained at 5% for both years. The greatest change was in government salaries at 10% in 1990, twice that of the 1980s. (161 words.)

Now summarise in your owns words, use synonyms to help paraphrase your answer. **Tip**, do not simply repeat the model task. The data given here is for practice purposes only. You have 20 minutes.

The two charts show the budget for the London Borough of Greenwich in both 1980 and 1990

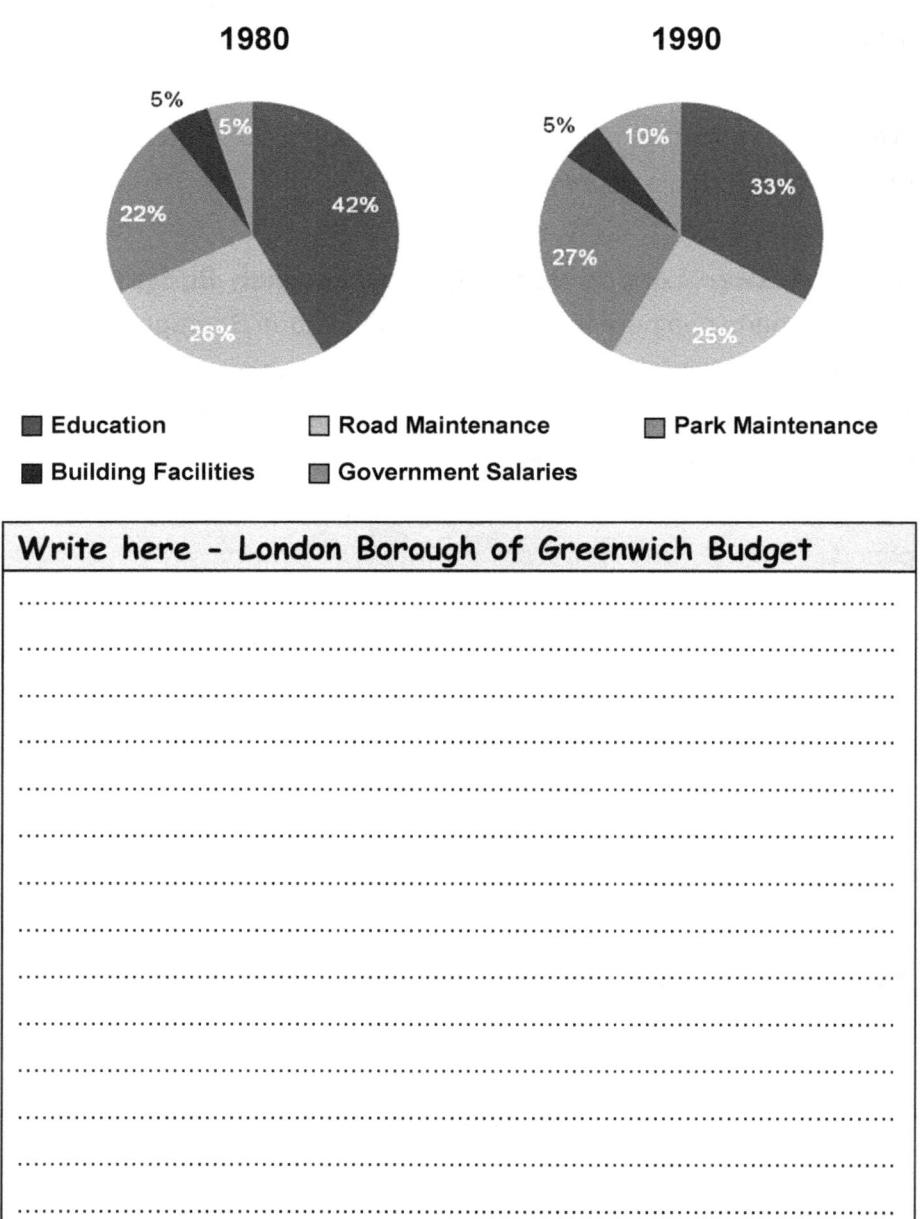

Write here - London Borough of Greenwich Budget

....
....
....
....
....
....
....
....
....
....
....
....
....
....
....
....

Task 2

You might be presented with a point of view, argument or problem. Take a look at the academic model for international corporations. Pay attention to the underlined keywords.

Write a report giving your opinion of international corporations. You must write at least 250 words in about 40 minutes.

Model Answer International Corporations

These days, international corporations find it <u>effortless</u> both to sell their <u>goods</u> all around the world, and establish <u>factories</u> wherever it is convenient. I believe this has a <u>damaging</u> effect on humanity's quality of life in three specific areas.

My first concern relates to their goods. International corporations and supporters of global economies argue these companies produce high-quality goods for more people. Conceivably, there is some measure of truth to this, but it indicates that consumers have fewer choices of goods to <u>purchase</u>. When dominant international corporations saturate local economies with their discounted-products, they force the <u>collapse</u> of local businesses that have smaller bankrolls resulting in limited choices of products.

The second point is openness. It is sometimes believed that international corporations globalise communities and provide more openness. This may be true. However, I would <u>contend</u> that many civilizations in fact lose their cultural diversity. If consumers bought <u>a variety of</u> goods, communities <u>around the globe</u> could be different. The evidence seems striking, as many consumers shop in <u>identical</u> grocery chains and buy similar goods.

Finally, numerous supporters for these international corporations often argue they <u>contribute to</u> local employment. Although, this is undeniably true, it also reflects our <u>reliance</u> on them, which in turn makes us more defenseless to their actions. When corporations relocate their factories to other jurisdictions, this impacts local economies and employment.

Overall, I think consumers must demand action from governments to protect local communities from globalisation and ensure corporations are answerable for their decisions. We can utilize the benefits without the disadvantages and keep local businesses. (260 words)

As a **strategy**, identify keywords that express a general opinion or idea. For instance, *a lot of people believe that international corporations help provide more openness.* **Tip**, in academic writing it is more appropriate to write in a formal prose using the following structure: Noun + passive + clause. *It is believed that international corporations help provide more openness.*

Other verbs that take this form include:
argue, speculate, contend, report, agree, and many more which are not listed here.

Now rewrite the model answer, replace all underlined words with synonyms and paraphrase your response. Remember, do not repeat the model exactly. **Tip**, rephrase and restate the task. The opinion presented in this exercise is for practice purposes only. You have 40 minutes.

Write here - International Corporations

Rules and examples to help make simple sentences

To make a sentence you need three things:

1. A group of words in a sentence that makes sense on its own.

The first example below represents a sentence. You can understand what it means. It makes sense on its own. The second group of words don't make any sense, this isn't a sentence.

- *I parked my car next to my house.*
- *Cake, car, apartment, table, on Friday.*

2. When writing, use the right sentence punctuation.
Using punctuation will show the person who is reading your writing where the sentences begin and end.

- A sentence must begin with a capital letter.
- A sentence must end with a full-stop (.), a question mark (?), or an exclamation mark (!).

Caution!
Sometimes candidates confuse the punctuation to use at the end of a sentence. You can use commas (,), colons (:) or semicolons (;) in your writing, but they should never be used instead of a full-stop.

3. A sentence also needs to contain a subject and a verb.

- A sentence must have a **subject.** This is the person, or the thing, that is doing the verb. Example: *I, people, Friday, dog, you, table, the weather.*

- A sentence must also have a ***verb*** (a doing word).
  Example: *like, is, cooking, walked, need*.

Take a look at these example sentences that have highlighted ***subjects*** and ***verbs***:

- Last month **Aaron painted** the pub.
- **Friday was** a hot and sunny day.
- **Erin, be** quiet.
- **Are you** hungry yet?

Other Points to Note about Sentences

Sentences can either be very short or very long. There is no correct number of words to use in a sentence. Therefore, the length of the sentence depends on what you want to say, and the desired effect on your readers. **Tip**, when your sentences run too long, ensure that you haven't put several sentences together as one.

Unlike notes or lists of things to do that don't require sentences, it's important to remember that academic and business writing always requires structured sentences.

How to Put Simple Sentences Together

Constant use of short sentences can be a bit strange to read.
To make your writing more interesting, you can use two other sorts of longer sentences. The simplest of these is the **compound sentence**.

How do I make a compound sentence?

When you have two or more short, independent, simple sentences which are of **equal weight** you can join them together using special words called **coordinating conjunctions**. Example: *'I hate curry.'* is a simple sentence. *'I like Thai food.'* is also a simple sentence. You can write these together to make one, longer and more interesting compound sentence using a conjunction as in the following: *'I hate curry'* + **but** + *'I like Thai food'* = *'I hate curry, but I like Thai food.'*

- Junctions join two or more roads together, so we use conjunctions to join two or more short sentences together.
- Commas are **not** conjunctions and they should never be used to join short sentences together (commas aren't sticky, so you can't use them to stick information together!).
- These are the most common conjunctions: and, as, but, or, and so.
- Try to avoid using the same conjunctions repeatedly. It is much better to use a variety, mix and match as much as possible.

Tip, the conjunction that you use may change the meaning of your sentence! Conjunctions don't just stick sentences together; they show the **relationship** between the pieces of information.

Note the slightly different contextual meaning in the following sentences:

- I walked home. I was tired.
- I walked home and I was tired.
- I walked home as I was tired.
- I walked home but I was tired.
- I walked home so I was tired.
- I walked home or I was tired.

The final sentence, using **or** doesn't really make much sense. You can't use every coordinating conjunction everywhere - so choose wisely!

Keep in mind that compound sentences are simple elements joined together; they must make sense with or without conjunctions. Review the following example compound sentences:

- The train was crowded, **for** the weather was terrible.
- The coffee was hot, **and** I enjoyed the rich coffee taste.
- I don't usually get up at 7 a.m., **nor** do I get up at 5 a.m.
- I waited for the plane, **but** the plane was late.
- You can leave a message, **or** you can call back later.
- The heater is on, **yet** the room is still cold.
- The plane was delayed, **so** I had a cup of coffee.

Tip, think of the acronym "**FANBOYS**" to help you remember conjunctions. Now, let's discuss complex sentences for more clarity.

How do I Make a Complex Sentence?
Complex sentences aren't the same as compound ones. Complex sentences don't just divide into neat, complete, simple sentences if you take out the conjunctions. In complex sentences the conjunction is used to join together **clauses**. A clause is a group of words that contains a subject and a verb. Some of these clauses might be complete short sentences, but in a complex sentence at least one of them will **depend on the conjunction for its meaning**. In other words, if you take the conjunction away, the sentence won't divide into complete units that make sense by themselves. Example 1: *'The dinner was burned because she had forgotten it.'* = *'The dinner was burned'* + *'because'* + *'she had forgotten it.'* This is a complex sentence.

The elements of this sentence are:

- *'The dinner was burned'* = complete, short sentence
- *'because'* = conjunction (joining word)
- *'she had forgotten it'* = subordinate clause. This doesn't make sense on its own. What had she forgotten? This is called a 'subordinate clause' because without the rest of the sentence it doesn't really make sense.

Example 2: *'Although I'm not very good, I really enjoy playing football.'* = *'Although'* + *'I'm not very good'* + *'I really enjoy playing football.'*

The elements of this complex sentence are:

- *'Although'* = conjunction (joining word). Yes, sometimes conjunctions can appear at the beginning of a sentence!
- *'I'm not very good'* = subordinate clause. This doesn't make sense on its own. What are you not very good at? This is called a 'subordinate clause' because without the rest of the sentence it doesn't really make sense.
- *'I enjoy playing football'* = complete short sentence.

Caution!

As for compound sentences, commas are **not** conjunctions and they should never be used to join short sentences or clauses together (commas aren't sticky, so you can't use them to stick information together).

Example: *'The dinner was burned, she had forgotten it.'* = incorrect. *'The dinner was burned **because** she had forgotten it.'* = correct.

The Important Connective Words

When you use **compound** and **complex** structures, this makes the sentences more interesting. For both of these, you need a good selection of **conjunctions**, or joining words.

The 'grand seven' conjunctions are:

The most frequently used
although, as, and, but, because, if, so

In addition to these seven, those for **time**, **place**, or **agreement** are also important.

Time
after, before, since, until, when, whenever, while

- **After** the election, Greg Robertson continued with Vision Vancouver to move the city forward.
- The Canucks failed **before** the final game finished.
- Vancouver has not been the same **since** the 2010 Olympics.
- The rain in Vancouver often continues **until** May.
- The students turned off the computers **when** the class had finished.
- The RCMP (Royal Canadian Mounted Police) often stop drivers **whenever** they suspect irregularities with the car registration.
- British Columbian kindergarten kids go to school **while** their parents work.

Place
Where, wherever

- The restaurant staff said we could sit **where** we wanted to.
- In the park, dogs tend to wander **wherever** they like.

Agreement
although, though, whether

- The education system in Japan yields students with high international recognition **although** changes to teaching methodology could enhance students' critical thinking.
- Japanese students can read English quite well **though** they have difficulty speaking it.
- It would be several weeks before the students knew **whether** they had passed their exams.

Remember!
Sentences that use a variety of conjunctions are far better than repeatedly using the same ones. In addition, keep in mind that conjunctions can also **change the meaning of the sentence**. You can't use every conjunction everywhere, so choose carefully. Well connected sentences will give you more points on the exam.

Common Connective Words Used in Writing

When IELTS candidates are taking the exam, they often do not join short sentences together correctly. The proper use of connective words, also known as transitional words, can transform your writing.

Try to use the connective words below in your sentences and become familiar with their use on all IELTS exam modules.

Common connective words indicating:

Addition	Consequence	Condition	Contrast
in addition	as a result	provided that	however
similarly	therefore	depending on	nonetheless
likewise	consequently	unless	alternatively
besides	admittedly	whether	but
furthermore	in that case	if	although
			whereas
Certainty	**Definition**	**Example**	**Reason**
undoubtedly	is refers to	for instance	because of
of course	means that is	such as	due to
obviously	consists of	to illustrate	in other words
certainly		for example	leads to
plainly		just as in	since
Sequence	**Summary**	**Time**	**Declaration**
first	to summarise	before	assert
second	in summary	since	argue
then	in conclusion	meanwhile	affirm
next	to recapitulate	at the moment	contend
after this/that	in short	when	claim
		as soon as	

6
Speaking

Speaking

Speaking Skills Practice

In the three parts of the speaking module, strategies for cognitive thinking and key words or sentences help you to answer questions more confidently. A good **strategy** to use before you speak is to give yourself 'rehearsal time' in your head. Try to think what you want to say by utilizing 'delaying sounds' like: 'er', which are used by native English speakers to give themselves time to compose responses.

In conversations give yourself extra thinking time by commenting on what the other person has said. For example:
"Yes, I think I agree with you but ..."
"Yes, that's a good question ..."

Try to avoid silences. Ask for repetition or explanation if you need it or even if you need time to think of your reply. Such as:
"I didn't quite get that, could you say it again?"

Tip, don't try to memorise responses but listen carefully to others and reuse their vocabulary or expressions if they are good. Try to speak as naturally as possible.

Introduction to IELTS Speaking

The general and academic modules for the speaking test are the same. The speaking module takes an average of 11-15 minutes to complete. The test is distinctive from other language exams, because you have your own one-on-one examiner. The examiner will ask you questions from those written on the "examiner frame". In the third part, the examiner has some control over the questions based on the level and skill that you have exhibited in the first two parts. The examiner records the conversation, so if the thought of this makes you nervous, practice with a recorder to become accustomed to the idea.

Part 1 - Questions about yourself and everyday situations

The examiner may be a man or a woman. Since experience indicates that examiners are more than likely to be women, we have used a female pronoun in this situation. The examiner will introduce herself. You must also be ready to reciprocate and introduce yourself as well. You will need to show your identification that matches the candidates' list. After, the examiner will ask some general questions about your family, food, school, work, neighbourhood, or other similar topics. This takes about 4-5 minutes and there is no preparation time.

Part 2 - Topic given by the examiner

Part 2 is sometimes referred to as the 'long turn'. You will be presented with a topic. There will be three questions related to the topic and one question about your opinion. In part 2 you have one minute to organise thoughts on the topic, and then you have around a minute to speak. When you have finished, the examiner will ask you one or two questions based on your response. **Strategy**, introduce the main concept to your talk using key words or phrases from the first sentence of the topic. **Tip**, talk continuously and spontaneously. Part 2 takes about four minutes and you have one minute of preparation time.

Part 3 - Conversation on abstract topics

The examiner may ask you questions based on the topic you have just talked about in part 2. The rationale for part 3 is to allow you to discuss abstract topics such as 'What is your opinion of ...?' or 'What would you do if ...?' Remember this should form part of a conversation, so you have to maintain the dialogue and keep it going.

Model Talk - National Holidays

In my opinion, national holidays are important because they help families to stay connected and provide an opportunity to celebrate a country's tradition. Holidays such as Christmas give us time to reconnect with distant relatives that we do not see so often. On these holiday occasions, families can share in special events like singing Christmas carols together and enjoying a game or two. These special moments can bind families together in a fun and interesting way. Traditional holidays also provide us with the opportunity to learn about customs and traditions established through the history of one's country. These nostalgic moments remind us of the importance and significance of our cultural heritage. A time to enjoy good food and happy moments. Remember, the actual speaking test lasts between 11-14 minutes.

Marking

Candidates are assessed on the following criteria:
- fluency and coherence.
- lexical resources.
- grammatical range and accuracy.
- pronunciation.

Fluency and Coherence

Fluency and coherence measures your ability to talk like a native speaker, and connect your ideas and thoughts without long pauses. Therefore, long 'ums' and silences will lose you points whereas 'Well, there was another issue I wanted to mention about that ... no, sorry, I've forgotten what I was going to say'. These pausing techniques are equivalent to the long 'ums' but demonstrate your language range to the examiner. Remember to use linking words such as 'after that', 'on the contrary' 'moreover' to help facilitate continuity.

Lexical Resource

Lexical resource has two elements to it, one that covers your range of vocabulary and two, dealing with your vocabulary gaps by organising your thoughts differently. At times you may find yourself searching for the right words if your vocabulary range is limited. Rather than long pauses, try to impress your examiner by saying the same thing another way. Take a look at this example, maybe you are familiar with the word 'stapler' but if for some reason you have drawn a blank, simply describe it like this 'the device used to bind material together'.

Grammatical Range and Accuracy

Grammatical range and accuracy also has two parts. Your grammatical range determines your ability to move between different tenses (for example, passives or perfect) and use various structures if needed to communicate your message effectively, and secondly how skillful you are with the transitions. Be careful to choose structures wisely as you don't want to show that can't handle the various forms correctly. Nonetheless, if you are confident and have a good range of grammatical structures, then by all means demonstrate you skill to the examiner.

Pronunciation

Pronunciation various from person-to-person so it is inevitable that you will have an accent. Accents reflect regional differences and where people come from. However, if your words are poorly pronounced or incomprehensible, or if your intonation, stress and rhythm come at the wrong place, then you will lose points.

Tips and Strategies for Speaking

The speaking strategies and tips below will help you to gather your thoughts and present ideas clearly.

A good **strategy** for part 1, know the vocabulary to talk about your hobbies and everyday situations. **Tip**, give clear succinct answers and explain your reasons, but don't try to memorise your responses. A good level of nouns and adjectives will facilitate your speaking with ease. Remember keep in mind that your ability to communicate ideas effectively is what the examiner is looking for. Avoid trying to impress the examiner if you are not confident in doing so. Focus on transmitting your ideas only.

In part 2, your **strategy** is to introduce the main idea to your talk using key words from the topic given to you. The main idea and keywords help you to focus clearly and will help guide the examiner through your ideas. **Tip**, talk spontaneously with a lot of variety in your words and structures. It is important to avoid using a prepared topic, the examiner will catch on if you try to change the subject to something you have prepared. The examiner will stop you when the time is up.

Time permitting, part 3 involves your opinion or response to questions that may relate to part 2. As a **strategy** mention your logic or rationale for opinions given, and elaborate as you talk. **Tip**, it is not important whether you believe the ideas presented, but rather you provide a rationale for both sides of an argument. At this stage of the exam, you should have some idea of how good your speaking is. When meeting face-to-face with the examiner don't look scared, as this will only show a lack of confidence in your ability. Finally, the test is 11-14 minutes and it assesses your language level you use to communicate.

IELTS Speaking Test Part 1

Familiar Topics

In this first part, the examiner might ask two or three questions on topics that relate to your hometown, family, food, work or study. Answers must be in sentences and fluent. Take a look at some of the common topics below and practise with your friends.

About Yourself and Everyday Situations

1. Questions About Your Hometown
- What kind of place is it?
- What's something interesting about it?
- Would you say it's a safe place to live?
- What changes would you like to see in your town?
- What's the main industry there?

Think about your answers and write them here
....
....
....
....
....
....

2. Questions About Your Work and Study

- What kind of job do you have?
- What's a usual day like at your job?
- What are some aspects of your job you don't like? Why?
- What are you studying at school/college? Why?
- What's your favourite subject? Why?

Think about your answers and write them here
....
....
....
....
....
....

3. Questions About Your Family and Food

- What's your family like?
- What do you like doing with your family? Why?
- What do you think about foreign food? Why?
- What's a typical meal in your family? Why?
- What kind of food do you like best? Why?

Think about your answers and write them here
....
....
....
....
....
....

Now practise with your friends on the topics below, and fill in the blank spaces with suitable words. Try to think of different words to use in each situation. Remember these are only possible situations, the examiner might also ask you to talk about hobbies or holidays.

Tell me something interesting about your hometown
A. I come from a 1 _____ village in 2 _____. We have just a few 3 _____ and a 4 _____. The nature is very beautiful and people are 5 _____. B. I come from a small town 1 _____ the main city. In the summer, there are 2 _____ festivals and 3 _____ events. It's an amazing 4 _____ to live.
Tell me something about your work or school
C. I work for a 1 _____ transportation company that delivers goods and products across 2 _____. In the town, a lot of people 3 _____ bicycles as these are cheaper than 4 _____. D. I'm studying 1 _____ at a local 2 _____. The classrooms are 3 _____ spacious, and the technology is 4 _____.
Tell me something about your family
E. I have a(n) 1 _____ sister only, so our family is 2 _____ small. Many of our relatives are scattered across the country, so it is very 3 _____ to see them. On special occasions we sometimes meet in the 4 _____ for dinner, but this depends 5 ____ everyone's schedule. F. I'm one of three siblings, so our family is large in comparison to others. We live in a big 1 _____ near the edge of the 2 _____. During the winter months we all go 3 _____ on the local mountains and 4 _____ ice skating sometimes at the 5 _____.

IELTS Speaking Test Part 2

Task Card on a Particular Topic (Long Turn)
After the examiner has given you a topic, you will have one minute to prepare your notes and ideas. In this part, you have to speak for 1 to 2 minutes fluently without stopping, talking and answering on about three points, and provide your opinion on the issue presented. The total task takes 3 to 4 minutes. Remember to identify keywords and introduce the main concept. Look at the following two examples below:

1) **Identified keywords** - *national holiday*
2) **Example introduction** - *National holidays in Japan often relate to nature, and Marine Day (Umi no Hi) is a day that celebrates the bountiful supply of fish from the ocean.*

1. Describe a national holiday
- what is the name of the national holiday?
- what time of the year is it?
- who do you celebrate it with?

Write your notes and ideas below
....
....
....
....
....
....

On the topic card you will see the phrase 'you should say' followed by three questions. Pay attention to the question words to help you focus.

2. Describe a teacher that changed your ideas
- who was the teacher?
- what caused the changes in your thinking?
- what subjects did you learn from this teacher?

Write your notes and ideas below
....
....
....
....
....
....

3. Describe a best friend
- how did you meet this friend?
- what kind of character does this friend have?
- why do you like spending time together?

Write your notes and ideas below
....
....
....
....
....
....

Note: You must provide sufficient information to answer the questions, but these don't need to be in detail. Once the IELTS test begins, you will not be permitted to write any further notes. It is prohibited to write in the booklet.

IELTS Speaking Test Part 3

General and Abstract Topic Discussion
In part 3, the examiner will ask you questions based on part 2. These questions facilitate the transition for this final stage and will help guide you to more abstract thinking. The examiner wants to know your opinions in relation to the part 2 topic. So, if the part 2 topic related to 'describing a teacher that changed your ideas', part 3 might be about teacher practices, modern education, technology in education, or the importance of education in the 21st century.

Possible Examples

Part 2 Topic	Part 3 Possible Abstract Topics
Describe your best friend	Do you think best friends are more important than family? Is friendship related to culture?
Describe a cultural event	What is the significance of cultural events? How are they celebrated across cultures?
Describe something you bought	Are people in your country wise? Are possessions the path to happiness?
Describe an important figure	What are the qualities of a good teacher or leader? Why are role models or heroes important?
Describe your family	What is the role of parents in raising a family? Who should be responsible for discipline?

1. How is Success Achieved?
Candidates achieve success when they:

- comment on the questions.
- give personal and longer answers.
- divide up their responses.
- use modals, the present, past, and future tenses correctly.

2. Comment on the Questions
- That's an interesting point of view. I saw a documentary about that last week.
- That's a significant issue today. Governments are constantly discussing that in their political agendas.
- Well, that might be difficult to predict. I'm not sure if anyone can really determine what is going to happen.
- Wow, that's a tough question. It really depends on your perspective.
- Absolutely, I've often considered that.

3. Give Personal and Longer Answers
- I think people need to have extracurricular activities, because it helps us relax more.
- In my case, I really like photography as it gives me a sense of freedom when I'm in nature.
- On the other hand, we must find a balance so that it doesn't interfere with our everyday tasks or living.
- I recall a situation where one of my university friends spent numerous hours surfing the Internet. In the end, he received much lower grades.

4. Divide Your Responses
- Basically, there are several ways to look at this issue. One way is to envisage ....
- I believe there are numerous approaches to resolve this problem. I think one would be to ....
- That depends on one's perspective. For instance, if you were company manager you would have one viewpoint, whereas if you were an employee you may have different attitude.
- Possibly, two different results could happen. First of all, there could be ....
- There have been a number of effects. One of these is that ....
- I would imagine that you could divide it up into two or three areas. First ....

5. Use Modals
- In part 1, the focus is on present tenses.
- Part 2 utilizes past tenses.
- Finally, part 3 focuses on the future tenses and modals.
- In part 3 you must be able to, and are expected to predict, analyse, relate, suggest and evaluate by giving your opinions using modals such as can, could, may, might and so on.

6. Common Phrases to Express Opinion
- Personally, I think ....
- I believe that ....
- In my opinion, ...
- In my view, ...
- I'd like to say that ....
- From my perspective ....
- It is said that ....

- Generally it is believed that ....
- Some universities say that ....
- In general it is considered that ...

Speaking Practice - Expressing Opinion
Personally, I think colleges should provide more technology in the classrooms **because** these days many students are tech savvy.
I believe that ....
In my opinion, ...
From my perspective ....
Some universities say that ....
Generally it is believed that ....
In general it is considered that ....

7
Review and Memorising

Review and Memorising

Review to Strengthen Weaknesses

As mentioned in the introduction, a study contract is important because it helps you use time effectively. Likewise, when reviewing, take a planned approach and focus on your weaknesses rather than perfecting your strong points. This will enable you to gain higher marks. Also, try to work with other candidates to gain  understanding of your strengths and weaknesses because in a group everyone can achieve more insight.

Multisensory Revision Strategies

Prior knowledge can play an important role in learning, so by linking your past educational and personal experiences you can learn through visual (seeing it), auditory (hearing it) and kinesthetic (doing it). Consider using pictures, charts, sound recordings, and movement to enhance your memory. First determine your strongest sensory input for learning. For example, if you learn better by seeing, use colours and words to create a mind-map, which can help expand your vocabulary. If you grasp ideas faster by listening, record your voice when reading text aloud and listen to it later at home, on a bus or train. Finally, if you are more of an active learner, try teaching your friends or acting out different scenarios to help you gain greater understanding of new knowledge presented.

Sharpen Vocabulary Memory

An important point to keep in mind with memory is that repetitive review does not lead to good memory; you must try to connect your experiences with new knowledge. When you can visualize images in your mind, you can connect ideas or concepts together. Try picture and words games for reviewing vocabulary. For example, use vocabulary picture cards to help prompt your memory. These cards often come with the vocabulary on the front and picture on the reverse side. Practise using a mind-map to extend your usage of word families such as relation, relative, relatively.

Enhance Grammar Understanding

Make a checklist for grammatical structures that you understand well and as you gain more confidence in using other patterns check them off. Focus on your weaker grammar areas and attempt to relate personal experiences to new knowledge that will facilitate better memory of structural forms.

Past Paper Resources

If you are diligent and time yourself, past exam papers are a useful method for reviewing. Let speaking practice be your motivator for success. The example past papers, which can be downloaded, help you to identify areas in need of attention.

Teacher and Friend Resources

Teachers and friends may well be an excellent resource for advice, so ask them for their input to your questions as part of the review process.

8
Study Tips

Study Tips

Ten Days to Go

Check your revision programme to ensure you have covered everything. Are there some areas that need reviewing? Make the most of this ten-day period to review and focus on your weak points.

Try reviewing without looking at your notes, especially areas that are difficult for you to remember.

Keep in mind that the examination is not focused on your notes, rather it assesses your English skills in reading, writing, listening and speaking. Try to take some time to enjoy English  in other ways such as watching films and listening to music.

Look back to when you began your studies for IELTS. Can you see improvements? Stay positive and celebrate your achievements.

 Think about the day of the examination and plan to wear something comfortable, an item of clothing that also makes it special. This clothing acts as your psychological state of readiness for the examination. Frequently rest and relax to avoid becoming apprehensive about the exam day. Apprehension reduces your cognitive ability to learn. Plan a regular exercise regime and incorporate some mini mental reviews while you workout such as phrasal verbs or compositional ideas.

Ensure you are familiar with the exam centre's location and the time required to arrive punctually. When travelling to the centre, come up with a good exam strategy.

The night before the examination avoid alcoholic beverages and relax as much as possible.

Examination Day

Prepare yourself mentally for this important day by wearing your chosen clothes and maintaining a positive attitude. Enjoy a hearty breakfast but avoid too much tea or coffee. Being comfortable while the exam is in progress is important for your success.

Review your schedule for the examination, make a note of the amount of time you will allocate to each question and remember to allow sufficient time for corrections.

Check that you have the same ID that was submitted with your application, and ensure you have enough pencils and paper.

While Taking the Examination

Concentrate on the task ahead and do not focus on any distractions. View time as your opponent, so watch it carefully and allow sufficient time to review and correct your responses. Without rushing, try to complete as many of the questions as possible.

9
General Information

General Information

IELTS Preparation - Speaking Test

The Examiner

- Examiners come from various English speaking countries.
- All examiners are licensed teachers with university degrees.
- The examiners want you to do well and will be patient with you.
- IELTS examiners have been given specialised training.
- Examiners assess you fairly even if they appear unfriendly.

The Examiner's Focus

- **Pronunciation** only becomes an issue if it interferes with communication, so it's important to speak with a clear voice.
- **Sentence structure** helps with the communication process and is one way to better improve your speaking score in a relatively short time.
- **Fluency and coherence** are extremely important, so make sure you speak coherently and don't have too many hesitations.

Score Results

- If you find it difficult to make good sentence structures, use too many hesitations and speak unclearly, you will only achieve band 4 or lower.
- In order to achieve band 5, some mistakes and hesitations are permitted but you must be able to easily produce simple structures without errors.

- To reach band 6 you must produce much longer sentences with fewer hesitations and use a variety of language patterns. At this stage some errors are acceptable as long as communication is clear but it is imperative to paraphrase.
- To get a chance at reaching band 7, you will need to increase your overall speed, improve your memory, understand what information the examiner is asking for, and use a variety of well-connected paraphrased sentences with fewer mistakes.
- If you can speak fluently and clearly on any topic, utilise a wide variety of vocabulary and structures with just minor errors, you might stand a chance achieving band 8.

Strategies for Speaking

Part 1

- In part one the questions are relatively easy, so this is your opportunity to impress upon the examiner. Remember, if you provide simple responses the examiner will not know if you are band 4 or 5. However, if you use coherence, clear pronunciation, numerous lexical resources, and correct grammar, the examiner might consider you to be at band 6 or 7.
- The **strategy** here is to use this time to focus on making good sentences. Waiting until part 2 or 3 will be too late and you might not do as well. Think of this time as your opportunity to warm up and sharpen your approach.

Part 2

- In part 2, the long turn, the examiner will provide you with a sheet of paper and a pencil to make notes. Remember you have just one minute, so use this time wisely to focus on your topic. As a **strategy** you could make a list of key words to guide your speaking. For example if your topic is music, conductor, orchestra, instruments, musicians, and concert hall would all relate to classical music. Candidates that fail to make notes often use too many hesitations such as 'uh', 'I think perhaps', 'um ..', 'well', and 'it seems to me'. These hesitations will only achieve a lower result. Use notes to help you remember more details.

- Preparation is the key to success. First, make one key *point* sentence. Then provide two to three sentences with your *rational*. Next, give an *example* and describe it using two to three sentences. Finally, restate your main *point* using a different sentence structure. This **strategy** leads to a *P.R.E.P* method for clearer communication.
- Practise is also key to your success. Select a topic, make notes for one minute, then make four to five sentences in two minutes using the PREP method. Try to practise this method every day until the test. Remember to time yourself.

Part 3

- The final and most challenging stage comes rapidly. At this stage you should be ready for the examiner's general questions in connection with your part 2 topic. This is your opportunity to expand your ideas further, so listen for the examiner's cue.
- Time your responses carefully and limit them to two sentences for each answer. If you talk too long, or your introduction goes on, the examiner might wonder whether you can answer the question or not.

- When responding, use a general to specific **strategy**. Once you hear the examiner's question, provide your general opinion on the topic then back it up with a specific rational in one to two sentences. Although not the focus, this will demonstrate to the examiner that you understand the question and can answer it sufficiently.

10
Speaking Exercises

Speaking Exercises

IELTS Preparation - Speaking Practice

Building Better Sentences

Question: Can you tell me something about your family?
Common response: There is my mother, father and myself.
Better answer: In Europe today, a majority of families have one or two children, but my family is the exception as I have two brothers.

Question: Can you describe your hometown?
Common response: My hometown is quite small.
Better answer: Although my hometown is small in comparison to other major cities, it has numerous distinctive advantages that make it a special place.

Question: What do you think about your language classes?
Common response: Studying a new language is difficult.
Better answer: When I think about the complexities of language, I feel as though it would be easier to give up, which is why I decided to study in the UK.

Question: What are your future aspirations?
Common response: I want to become a doctor.
Better answer: I often thought about being a doctor when I was younger as I like to help people, so as an adult I can see the future possibilities as my dream becomes a reality.

Question: What hobbies do you have?
Common response: I like to take photos and play basketball.
Better answer: My favourite hobby is taking photos of nature, and I also like to watch sports games and spend time chatting with my friends on weekends.

Question: What special festivals are there in your country?
Common response: The Tanabata Festival is popular in Japan.
Better answer: In the first week of August each year, the Tanabata festival celebrates two legendary stars that meet after being separated by the milky way.

Question: What are some of the common jobs in your country?
Common response: Many workers in Japan are company employees.
Better answer: Two of the biggest industries in Japan are telecommunications and cars, where a large number of people work in offices or factories across Japan.

Question: If you can study overseas, where would you go?
Common response: I want to go to Canada.
Better answer: If I am in a position to secure a student visa, I hope to study economics in Toronto, Canada, and then I can return to London and work for a successful accounting firm.

Question: Can you describe your typical day?
Common response: I get up at 7 am and go to work.
Better answer: I usually get up at 7 am, take a shower, have breakfast then leave for work around 8 am to catch a bus across the street.

Connecting Sentences

As with writing, when you speak try to connect your sentences to show transition and logical flow. Correct use of connective or transitional words demonstrates to the examiner how well you can express ideas, show a shift in thought, or contrast a given argument. Use connective words sparingly, otherwise your speech might sound unnatural. Review the connective word list below to help you gain better understanding and usage for all parts of the IELTS speaking module.

After or before

- After we finished, we watched T.V.
- Before we can go home, we must tidy up.
- After that, I went to work.
- Before that, I was eating breakfast at home.

Although or even though

- Although I live in a small house, it's very cozy.
- Even though my house is on a busy street, I like the area a lot.

Another

- Another good point about my school is its location.
- Another way to succeed on IELTS would be to practise more.

As with or just like

- As with your first example, we should consider this one equally.
- Just like China, India has a booming economy.

At the same time

- In the winter I wanted to ski every day. At the same time, I realised I need to study more.
- These days there are too many cars on the road. At the same time, governments are expanding public transportation.

Besides or in addition to

- Besides that point, there's another interesting factor that comes to mind about traffic congestion.
- In addition to that motor vehicle act, there are numerous laws to reduce the possibility of accidents.

But

- World climates may have changed due to fossil fuel usage, but in my opinion industrialisation is important for progress.
- In most situations that is true, but air pollution affects human health which can also interfere with economic growth.
- Countries around the globe are trying to limit their carbon emissions, but I personally feel this is too late.
- In an ideal world we might live pollutant free, but the costs would seem outrageously expensive.

Because

- Many people believe that independence creates wealth. I disagree because unity bonds us together for sustainable solutions and social harmony.
- In my opinion, poverty is caused by big corporations because they tend to out-compete smaller businesses and farmers.

Except for
- Except for that one occasion, I can't think of any other issue.
- Except for the weather, the holiday was fantastic.

For example
- Standardized tests cannot always produce an accurate picture of students' ability. For example, these tests only measure academic ability and not employable skills.
- Education provides economic stability for families and society. For example, graduates can secure better jobs and contribute to society through taxation.

However or yet
- I think you are correct. However, from another perspective it could be viewed this way.
- The universe is both ancient and vast. Yet I wonder if life exists beyond earth.

Rather than
- Rather than trying to memorise details for the IELTS exam, use strategies for better success.
- Rather than tolerate the office politics, I decide to transfer to another branch.

The reason is
- I don't agree with that analysis. The reason is that it implies there is only one possible solution to the problem.
- The reason I doubt that hypothesis is neutrinos have mass subatomic particles formed by the sun's natural decay.

This or that

- This is a great place to live, even better than I imagined it would be because the streets are lined with beautiful trees.
- Not only is science interesting, but it is also very fascinating.
- That was a good film, but not as good as the original production made several years ago.
- I've heard it said that world economies are linked to multinational corporations, and I have to agree with that because it appears that money is a motivator.

When or whenever

- When I consider the possibilities of education, I think about my future success and where I can work and live.
- Whenever I take a train, I often think about the nostalgic journeys I took with my father as a boy.

General to specific sentences

In order to move beyond band 4 or band 5, candidates need to provide some explanation that follows opening statements. Sentences like **this company is important, or I love sushi** are too simple. (Very general.) You need to explain why the company is important and why you love sushi. For instance, **this company is important because it supports local farmers and workers.** (This is a very specific sentence.) Or, I love sushi for its delicious taste. (Specific reason.)

Let's examine some other examples of general to specific sentences to facilitate higher Band scores.

- Switzerland is a convenient place to live. (General)
- Because it is central to Italy and Southern France, which makes it convenient for travel between these countries. (Specific)

- Hong Kong is my most favourite city in the world. (General)
- I not only enjoy its culture, but the dynamic life and food that makes it an interesting place for holidays. (Specific)

- I want to study English in Australia next year. (General)
- If I can obtain a working holiday visa for Australia, I will work in a tranquil location and study English in the nearest city to enjoy life to the fullest. (Specific)

Paraphrasing Sentences

When words seem to escape your mind, try to use other ways to explain what you want to say. There are five different **strategies** that can have an impact your spoken ideas to yield higher scores. Try to use:

1) easy words to express your ideas.
2) synonyms and antonyms.
3) comparisons.
4) examples or instances.
5) disagreement to show something is incorrect.

For example, a lion is a dangerous creature. This sentence is too simple and doesn't paraphrase what a lion is as there are many dangerous creatures that exist. In this case try to think about the whole creature such as size, number of legs, running speed and possible harm if snared by it. You can also use paraphrasing to provide more details for single nouns as in the example below that clarifies what as lion is:

- A lion is a large, four-legged creature that can run at speeds of up to 50 miles an hour and is potentially dangerous if snared by it.

Practise paraphrasing and adding more details

I got a good IELTS score.
....
....
My friend was late for class.
....
....
The weather is beautiful today.
....
....
It's a good day for ice cream.
....
....
I feel hungry.
....
....

Speaking Tasks

During the final stage of the IELTS exam, the part 3 speaking test, candidates will need to demonstrate their skills in using twelve different tasks.

These tasks include the following essential abilities:

- providing personal information
- giving general information.
- expressing preferences.
- narrating.
- comparing and contrasting.
- suggesting.
- expressing opinions.
- justifying opinions.
- speculating.
- analysing.
- summerising.
- conversation repair.

Providing personal information

- I was born in Spain and have lived in London since 1998.
- Currently all my family still live there, but I chose to study English in London.

Giving general information

- I live in a large flat with my friends, just outside London.
- London has many beautiful parks and areas to rest and relax.

Expressing a preference
- I prefer mangoes to apples because they are sweeter.
- I would sooner have been relaxing on a beach than shopping.

Narrating
- During my trip to Belgium in 2007, I went to Bruges.
- When I was at university last year, I gave a presentation on linguistics.

Comparing and contrasting
- Spain is not as good as France because the food is too oily.
- In comparison to Japanese food, Western food is often too rich.

Suggesting
- Perhaps it would be a good idea to rent a car for our holiday.
- One possible solution to unemployment might be to offer businesses tax free concessions.

Expressing opinions
- After careful consideration, it appears me that it would be much better to eliminate tax on food.
- After reading numerous articles on teaching methodology, in my opinion a differentiated classroom helps enhance student abilities.

Justifying opinions

- The reason for eliminating of tax on food, is that I believe it would provide families with more opportunities to eat nutritiously.
- As argued by many educators, there is an overwhelming amount of information to support use of technology in classrooms.

Speculating

- I'm uncertain about global warming trends, but it seems the Arctic circle may completely melt in the future.
- If weather conditions prevail, winters might become warmer.

Analysing

- When analysing data, one needs to carefully consider all relevant details, first of which are the data sources.
- There are numerous points to take into consideration when carrying out scientific research. First, we must determine the kind of data required and how to present it.

Summerising

- In conclusion, this book provides opportunities to develop strategies that help achieve cognitive success.
- When considering all the strategies and tips presented, take advantage of every opportunity that can facilitate improvement in your English skills.

Essential conversation repair or paraphrasing

- Perhaps I haven't presented my idea clearly. What I'm saying is, the solar ice caps are melting and winters could become a lot warmer in the future.
- In other words, with the reduction of the North and South poles, world climates will inevitably increase.

Final Strategies

Time is your biggest challenge

- Time cannot be stressed enough, so when you practise at home or school note the time for each session to gain some idea of your efficiency. Make sure you wear a watch to the exam and monitor your time carefully.

A state of preparedness is essential

- On the day of the exam you will not have time to think about your strategies, so being prepared now can facilitate your state of readiness. Plan, do, review and review again to sharpen your skills.

Cognitive practice is necessary

- The IELTS exam could be compared to an obstacle course in which you must navigate to succeed. Practicing is necessary to increase your cognitive abilities that sharpen your skills.

Randomly guessing to achieve better scores

- An unanswered question yields zero, but guessing can improve your score significantly to increase your chances of success.

11
Appendix 1
Answer Keys

Appendix 1 Answer Keys

Keyword identification

Planning and Evaluation

	Question 1		Question 2
A	direction	A	focused
B	dictate	B	merging
C	translates	C	needs

Life Long Learning UK

	Question 1		Question 2
A	September	A	reforming
B	development and definitions	B	statutory
C	set out to raise	C	comply

Vocabulary

Describing & Analysing Tables or Graphs

| 1.D | 2.J | 3.H | 4.G | 5.A | 6.I | 7.B | 8.E | 9.C | 10.F |

Words related to media

| 1.C | 2.G | 3.F | 4.A | 5.B | 6.H | 7.I | 8.E | 9.J | 10.D |

Words related to Work or Employment

| 1.J | 2.A | 3.D | 4.H | 5.B | 6.I | 7.C | 8.F | 9.G | 10.E |

Words related to Money & Finance

| 1.G | 2.D | 3.J | 4.I | 5.H | 6.C | 7.F | 8.B | 9.E | 10.A |

Words related to Business & Finance

| 1.B | 2.E | 3.I | 4.A | 5.C | 6.J | 7.H | 8.D | 9.G | 10.F |

Words related to Geography

| 1.H | 2.G | 3.A | 4.I | 5.B | 6.E | 7.C | 8.J | 9.D | 10.F |

Words related to Architecture and Housing

| 1.E | 2.I | 3.J | 4.H | 5.C | 6.G | 7.F | 8.B | 9.D | 10.A |

Listening summary gap-fill

Shopping in Morocco and the US

	Question 1		Question 2
A	very different	C	open-air market

	Question 3		Question 4
A	fresher in Marrakech	B	more expensive

	Question 5		Question 6
A	negotiate the terms of a sale	C	fixed

Skim Reading

London Congestion Charge

Questions	
1.B	In the article's first paragraph, it states that the congestion charge came into effect in February 2003.
2.B	The article doesn't give any information about a consultation with the residents.
3.A	In paragraph 3, the article outlines various methods of payment.
4.A	Paragraph 1 states that the charge was introduced to counter pollution levels and traffic congestion.
5.D	Although the article doesn't explicitly say, it is aimed at anyone who wants to know more about its purpose.
6.C	As the article provides factual information and tells you about something, it's informative.
7.D	For readers that require additional information, a phone number and web site address is given in the last paragraph.
8.B	Paragraph 5 outlines how the entire system is monitored by cameras to check whether drivers have paid.
9.A	The article states that maps are available from various sources, including online.
10.C	The days and times the congestion charge is enforced are explicitly stated in paragraph 3.

Speaking Part 1

About Yourself Everyday Situations

Tell me something interesting about your home town

	Possible answer	Alternative answer
A.1	small	large
A.2	Nepal	Japan
A.3	shops	schools
A.4	petrol station	community centre
A.5	friendly	kind
B.1	close	near
B.2	many	a lot of
B.3	special	barbecue
B.4	place	convenience

Tell me something about your work or school

	Possible answer	Alternative answer
C.1	national	local
C.2	Asia	North America
C.3	ride	use
C.4	public transport	cars
D.1	law	business
D.2	college	university
D.3	quite	very
D.4	up-to-date	very new

Tell me something about your family

	Possible answer	Alternative answer
E.1	older	younger
E.2	quite	small
E.3	difficult	hard
E.4	city	town
E.5	on	upon
F.1	farmhouse	house
F.2	village	town
F.3	snow boarding	skiing
F.4	enjoy	go
F.5	rink	skating centre

12 Appendix 2 Resources

Appendix 2 Resources

Online Resources

BBC Learning English - Listening
http://www.bbc.co.uk/worldservice/learningenglish/general/sixminute/2014/09/140918_6min_london_skyline.shtml

BBC Learning English - Grammar and Pronunciation
http://www.bbc.co.uk/worldservice/learningenglish/grammar/pron/

British Council - Listen and Watch
http://learnenglish.britishcouncil.org/en/

British Council - IELTS Practice Materials
http://learnenglish.britishcouncil.org/en/ielts

British Council - Take IELTS Practice Tests
http://takeielts.britishcouncil.org/prepare-test/free-practice-tests

Canada Visa - IELTS Practice Tests and Band Score Calculator
http://www.canadavisa.com/ielts/free-practice-tests.html

IELTS - Sample Materials
http://www.ielts.org/test_takers_information/test_sample.aspx

Saone Education - Example Writing Papers
http://www.saonedu.org

Schools where you can study English

Australia

Euro Centres
http://www.eurocentres.com/en/language-school-sydney?gclid=COL17YSJg8ECFQMJvAodYLYAsQ

UNSW Institute of Languages
http://www.languages.unsw.edu.au/courses/part-time-english/?gclid=CLPKhraJg8ECFYqTvQodiH0AnA

Canada

University of British Columbia
http://www.eli.ubc.ca/

Vancouver Community College
http://www.vcc.ca/programscourses/program-areas/english-as-a-second-language/

United Kingdom

University of Greenwich
http://www2.gre.ac.uk/students/international/international-students/courses/pre-sessional

12
Bibliography

Bibliography

Biscuit Software Ltd. (2006). *International English Language Testing System.* Retrieved from http://www.english-online.org.uk/exam.htm

Education, P. (2006). *Longman essential activator* (2nd ed.). Harlow, Essex: Pearson Education ESL.

IELTS Institutions. (2013). *What is the test format?* Retrieved from http://www.ielts.org/institutions/test_format_and_results/what_is_the_test_format.aspx

IELTS Help Now. (2012, Nov 11). Retrieved from http://www.ieltshelpnow.com/iqs/dbitemid.5/sfa.view/rp.1/blog.html

Kennedy, K. (2010). *IELTS pathway to success: Cognitive study guide.* Japan: Alpine Publishing.

Lonsdale, C. (2006). *The third ear.* Hong Kong: Inkstone Books.

Microsoft Corporation. (2014). *Back to school with office clip art and media.* Retrieved from http://office.microsoft.com/en-us/images/back-to-school-with-office-clip-art-and-media-HA010237914.aspx

Pidgeon, C. (2011). *Congestion charge.* Retrieved from https://www.tfl.gov.uk/modes/driving/congestion-charge

Transport for London. (n.d.). *Paying the congestion charge*. Retrieved from https://www.tfl.gov.uk/modes/driving/congestion-charge/paying-the -congestion-charge

University College London. (2003, June 24). *Connectives and logic*. Retrieved from http://www.phon.ucl.ac.uk/home/dick/tta/connectives/connectives.htm

www.ingramcontent.com/pod-product-compliance
Lightning Source LLC
Chambersburg PA
CBHW070458090426
42735CB00012B/2607